# Ho

# Guided Life

## Meeting the Real YOU

channeled from my
Spirit Guide
Angels

**Book 2**

by

# LINDA DEIR

GUIDED Press

2675 W. Hwy 89A, PMB 1310,
Sedona, Arizona 86336
http://www.GuidedPress.com

Copyright © 2015 by Linda Deir
http://www.LindaDeir.com

Published in the United States of America by
GUIDED Press

Library of Congress Cataloging-in-Publication
Data
Deir, Linda; How to Live a Guided Life series,
Meeting the Real YOU, Book 2, channeled from
my Spirit Guide Angels is a compilation of
channeled insights that come through from
Linda's *Spirit Guide Angels* each week. These
are the same *Spirit Guide Angels* who have
stood by Linda and guided her since she was a

baby. At the end of each insight Linda explains:
HOW IT WORKS

Editor: Ray Holley
Interior design and layout: Linda Deir
Cover design: Linda Deir


First Edition, 2015
ASIN: B017JCO174 (Guided Press)

# TABLE OF CONTENTS

Title Page
Copyright
Foreword

Chapter 1 – RELEASE ALL RESISTANCE                                1
Your Resistance Creates Your Suffering
Living A Guided Life Is A Process
Solid As A Rock
The Fear Of Being Here

Chapter 2 – TRUTH IS YOUR CLEAN SLATE                        7
There Are Only Two Important Things in Your World
Liars Exposed
Enlightenment Happens When You Become
Comfortable With Being Uncomfortable

Chapter 3 – FIND YOUR PURPOSE, FIND
YOURSELF                                                                          13
Making The World A Better Place
The Real Meaning Of Normal
Why Your Are Here
What Creates Your Life

Chapter 4 – GUIDANCE REMOVES ALL
STRUGGLE                                                                         21
A Worthwhile Relationship
Miracles Are Common For *Us*
*We* Are Here When You Are Ready
You Can't Outsmart The Present Moment
Who Is It That's Guiding You?

**Chapter 5 – TRUST IS NATURAL WHEN YOU KNOW YOURSELF**     **29**
How To Look At Tragedies
Everyone Big And Small Needs To "Feel Loved"
Your Awareness Is Always ON

**Chapter 6 – ANXIETY – THE CONNECTION BREAKER**     **35**
Holding Your Breath Breaks Your Connection To *Us*
Staying Out Of Karmic Jail
The Source Of Your Unhappiness
Abandon Feelings Of Lack

**Chapter 7 – BELIEFS ARE LIKE GLASS, THEY SHATTER WHEN BROKEN**     **43**
Why Do You Believe What You Believe?
To Believe Or Not To Believe
You Are Intelligent Energy Wanting To Express Itself
The Yearning Of Your Soul Drives The Learning
Be Someone You Would Like To Be

**Chapter 8 – THE MEANING OF YOUR LIFE IS WHY YOU ARE HERE**     **53**
A Meaningful Life Will Be Your Masterpiece
Who You Really Are You Keep Hidden
Nothing Is Impossible
The Story Of Your Life
Live The Magic Ride Of Your Life

**About The Author**
**A Note from Linda Deir**
**Linda's Other Books**

# FOREWORD

## NOTE: The use of italics.

 The italic text following this ICON are all the insights "channeled from my *Spirit Guide Angels*," including my reference to my *Spirit Guide Angels* throughout the book.

In this book, you will learn about who the real you is, as seen through the eyes of your *guides*. It's your time to come out of hiding. In fact, there's never been a better time than right now to be "you," your real self.

Everything you have been told and were expected to be have never felt right to you. This just made you feel like someone who wasn't good enough already. Like something has been wrong with you. It's obvious that this doesn't, and never has worked for you. It hasn't worked for anyone.

Your *spirit guides* are eager to guide you back to "you." *They* have watched you get lost. You are becoming the person, the real you, the one who could do anything once you got here; that is until those who were already here told you differently. In reality, there's nothing you can't have or do when you walk with your *guides* by your side.

**Letting "You" Out of Hiding**

This book is a guide to help you break out of the old ways of thinking and doing things. Your perceptions will change as you begin to see what's really going on in your life and the world you live in.

It's time to let your real self come out of hiding. It's time to breathe like never before. It's time to meet you for the first time ever.

"You" have been feeling restless. That feeling is coming directly from the real "you," the one who came here to live the life you intended. This "you" couldn't allow you to forget the "you" who resides under the surface of everything you do. This repressed "you" who has wanted to come out since the first day you arrived is ready to fulfill your intentions when you are ready. This explains the void you are now feeling. The "you" of you has made itself known by making you feel a longing that something has been missing. The real "you" is relentless and will never give up on you. Once you let the real "you" out of hiding you will never be able to go back to just living a shadow of what used to be you ever again.

This is a big event, possibly the biggest event in

your lifetime. There are no role models for this, which is why you will need to enlist the help of your *spirit guides* and *angels*. *They* are *the only ones* who are truly qualified to guide you back to your authentic self who arrived here on that very first day. The irresistible urge that brought you here into this lifetime who knew you could do anything once you got here. This is who you really are and who it is you are about to meet, maybe for the first time in your life!

## How It Works

The more your connection with your *spirit guides* grows, the more you will see everything for what it is while learning who you really are. This is when you become more like *them*, your *spirit guide angels*. *They* see everything for what it is all of the time. You are just beginning to see what *they* see. *They* know everything about you, why you are here and what you intended to accomplish in this lifetime. Having *them* by your side to guide you, is not an option.

Making "room in your life" to receive *their* guidance will become imperative. Your line of communication with *them* becomes stronger as you become more authentic. That's when your *spirit guides* are able to reach you. That's the beacon that draws *them* to the real you.

## Becoming the Real You

As you are becoming the real you, not the you everyone says you are or expects you to be, but the person you are just beginning to discover yourself, people will think that something is wrong with you. The truth is that, for the first time in your life, nothing is wrong with you. You are just now becoming authentically you.

Attempting to explain this to the people who knew you as the person they expected and needed you to be will become an uphill battle. They were in your life because you, who didn't know yourself yet, willingly lived up to their expectations of who they needed you to be, for them. This may be the hardest adjustment you will have to make as you continue to become more of who you really are. Once you start on this path, you, the real you, can never go back to just being what others insisted that you be for their benefit. That's an acting job. So just because you've changed, don't expect everyone else to. There's nothing wrong with them and you can't pull them along if they don't get it.

## The Flip Side

Seeing things for what they really are and being who you really are will not be popular. In fact, if you voice your opinion about how you, the real you, sees things now, you will be viewed as an oddball by most people. They will look at you like you don't get it. You won't be cool or fit in anymore. I'm telling you this so you won't be disappointed when you start making progress only to find this out later on when it's too late and you can't go back.

I have seen so many people dive into this and become lost once they realized the consequences of the flip side. They actually believed that something was wrong with them and because of that they got more lost than they were before they started on their path. Their connection to their *spirit guides* and *angels* was not strong enough or long enough to avoid the self-doubt they fell into. Their fears instantly interrupted them; stopped them from believing in themselves and experiencing new things. No one warned me either, but I had an advantage from the time I was a baby. I have always had this ongoing relationship with my *spirit guide angels*.

Being different has always been more than okay with me since the benefits far outweighed the price I paid for being the oddball that many people labeled me as being.

Seeing things for what they really are will not always be easy. It's the truth, and the truth is not popular. If the truth were popular there wouldn't be so much deception in the world. That's also why there's a scarcity of love, real love. So while so many people are starving for love, they really have it backward. It starts with the truth, it starts with you.

**Putting it All Together**

So weigh the consequences of living a safe okay life versus a meaningful one. Either way, there will be consequences.

Choosing a meaningful life will require that you make room in your life for it.

- Don't expect others to be happy for you or understand.
- Stay true to yourself as your connection with your *spirit guides* and *angels* develops.
- You will no longer just be stuck here, doing time like most people.
- You will learn, know and understand anything you need at just the right time because you have your *guides* guiding you every step of the way.

By the way, there is no safe okay life anymore. A major shift is underway and since you are here you intended to be part of this. If you are feeling uneasy, then that's your *guides* nudging you to make a course correction. Everything you feel is coming from that *divine truth*. Trust it and let it guide you.

# Chapter 1 - RELEASE ALL RESISTANCE

## *Your Resistance Creates Your Suffering*

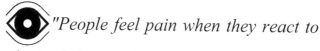 *"People feel pain when they react to physical harm. But when they react to mental harm it results in resistance to what's occurring naturally.*

*This resistance coming from your mind creates suffering. Suffering continues as long as you resist. If you resist all the time and can't stop it you will become fearful of the future and receive more stress. So when someone tells you to be "in the moment" what they are saying is to be in the flow of things as they happen naturally without resisting.*

*The best example is water. Water is soft and flexible and it resists nothing. It only goes with the flow. However, water contains much powerful energy and can wear anything down as it flows over it, even solid rock. So allow yourself to be in the flow like water and do not resist anything. Allow life to happen."*

**HOW IT WORKS:** In addition to the stress that resistance causes, it also causes worry and panic. You must break the cycle of resistance. People who do not break the cycle of resistance say things like they "hit rock bottom." Others just give up altogether, which isn't going with the flow at all, but sinking. Resistance is an automatic response to something you cannot control. The rock in the river has no control over the water flowing over it as it wears the rock down; even the strongest resistance to something will not win out in the end.

## *Living a Guided Life is a Process*

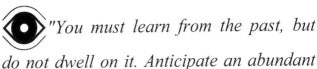*"You must learn from the past, but do not dwell on it. Anticipate an abundant future, but do not worry about it. Never try to force a future outcome.*

*We are walking with you in the present and are always guiding you. Living a guided life is a process that's always going on. You are always being guided.*

*Asking and listening in the present is what clears your path to the future. You must willingly tolerate all the lessons along the way as you become stronger from them on our walk together."*

HOW IT WORKS: Do you know how to anticipate an abundant future without interfering with it? This means you must allow it to unfold as a process and not chase it. Reaching that abundant future is like an obstacle course that involves lessons personal to you so you can achieve wholeness. In reaching the future that you envision, you must become the person it takes to achieve it.

## *Solid as a Rock*

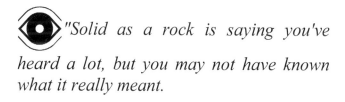 *"Solid as a rock is saying you've heard a lot, but you may not have known what it really meant.*

*To us, rocks are strong but not as indestructible as people think. Water running over a rock can shape it in any*

*way it wants. Eventually, the rock gives way and cannot hold its shape or form. This is similar to people trying to hold on as life wears them down.*

*Little by little, they try to hold on to their old ways but can't. Instead, the flow of life wears them down no matter what they try to hold onto - their beliefs, their thoughts, their biases, and their past.*

*Hanging on and not asking us to help you move forward is a mistake. We are the guides that lead you up the mountain."*

HOW IT WORKS: When you find yourself struggling you are not in the flow, you are the rock. This will only wear you down and keep you stuck as the flow of life etches away at you. You are here to enjoy the ride and go with the flow, so enlist your *guides* to help you lighten up and move through your life like the water, not the stubborn and stuck rock.

## *The Fear of Being Here*

 *"In order to expand your awareness and grow, you must damper the influence and control your mind has over your actions and feelings. If you can't do this you are not focusing and listening to the silence. All new knowledge resides in the present moment. Instead, you are destined to repeat patterns and habits that did not serve you in the past. This will rob your future of the magic and joy of your journey.*

*The toughest times you will have in your life are when you step outside the present moment and into the distractions of your mind. This is when fears appear, you forget who you are, your mind takes over your life like an auto-pilot and we watch you get lost again."*

HOW IT WORKS: To step into this higher way of living, you must be determined to overcome the mind's control and influence it has had over your experiences here. Stop making this experience so real. This is not all there is.

To begin, release your attachment to what others may think or do. You did not come here to sacrifice your life so you could please others. When you take the bold actions to step into this expanded awareness, it will be you that you find there first. The first few times this happens it may surprise you so much that it takes you right out of that magical moment. The sooner you repeat the steps that took you there, the quicker you will master this until you control your mind, and not the other way around. This is when you overcome the fear of being here so you can begin to live the life you intended before you arrived.

# Chapter 2 - TRUTH IS YOUR CLEAN SLATE

## *There Are Only Two Important Things In Your World*

*"We would tell you there are only two important things in your world - love and truth.*

*With "love" you can have caring, compassion, and respect for all that exists in your world. Without it you have the opposite, which is hatred. Hatred expresses itself in not caring about others, not showing compassion to people or animals, selfishness and all the needless suffering that results because of a lack of love.*

*The "truth" is self-evident. It is what's true in everything you do. The opposite of truth is lying. Lying for some has become an art form. Everything from little white lies to the most powerful people in the world lying to their citizens and other countries.*

*In between there's a lack of trust and emotion. Lying leads to all the troubles that exist today. If there were just these two things, love, and truth, to follow as a guideline for your life there would be no wars, no famine, no poverty, and no sicknesses that couldn't be addressed.*

*We come from pure love and truth. It is our only option. When you walk with us you will learn how important these two things are."*

**HOW IT WORKS:** The truth and love are both painstakingly real. You must be 100-percent present to fully experience them. There can be no distractions, no manipulations or strategies to outsmart them, or pretending, or cheating. You must be fearless; you must be you, pure and simple.

## *Liars Exposed*

*"When you speak the truth you speak with love. They are closely related.*

*When you hear the truth you react*

*differently than when you realize someone is lying to you. You feel a comforting presence that you are safe with this person. This person poses no threat.*

*However, when someone lies or exaggerates you get a different feeling. You are not hearing the truth. You could be getting an opinion, a perspective, or their agenda.*

*Even the smallest truth creates great clarity while the smallest lie creates great distrust. The truth is singular while lies have many facets. Lies create darkness of the most unloving kind. The truth eventually reveals itself and brings you to the light. Love is truth and truth is love."*

**HOW IT WORKS:** Your *spirit guides* reside in a place where there are no lies. Because of this *they* can spot a lie the instant you tell one. *They* see that as you losing your way. *They* don't waste *their* energy trying to lie to anyone because *they* see everything for what it is - the truth. It really is simple when you live like your *guides*, in love and truth. It's where you came from and return to when moving on from this lifetime.

---

## *Enlightenment Happens When You Become Comfortable With Being Uncomfortable*

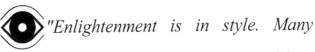*"Enlightenment is in style. Many books have been written about it and how to achieve it by modern day gurus.*

*Deep inside your consciousness is a silent stillness that is listening to, and observing the world without any "filters" to cloud "what is." It is a process of remembering all you forgot when you first came here. This is pure source energy.*

*Enlightenment unfolds gradually because if it happened all at once it would be a shock to your earthly ignorance. Enlightenment is realized through your work; like in the arts, music, writing, or any vocation that inspires you and enriches the lives of others, causing a ripple effect."*

10

**HOW IT WORKS:** The only way to reach enlightenment is to go with the flow. It's not something you decide to have or can chase. It's already there for you when you are ready to acknowledge it, step into it without hesitating, and go with the flow.

Like free-falling, it's a fearless excitement that once you do it a few times you will become comfortable with being uncomfortable, hence you start trusting the flow. This is the opposite of being dominated by an earthly ignorance.

# Chapter 3 - FIND YOUR PURPOSE, FIND YOURSELF

## *Making the World a Better Place*

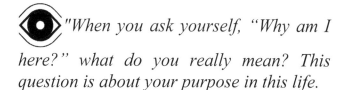*"When you ask yourself, "Why am I here?" what do you really mean? This question is about your purpose in this life.*

*We can tell you that the easy answer people give is to make the world a better place while you're here. That sounds surreal to many people because they don't know how to do that.*

*Asking "Why you're here?" means that you haven't found your purpose yet. We would tell you that you are here to use your gifts and talents that you brought with you. That is how you make the world a better place.*

*You see, your gifts and talents are who you are and what you have to share. They are not separate. What are you good at? How are you talented - maybe in many ways?*

*What are you happiest doing? What do you do well? Following the "what do I do well path," will lead you to satisfaction and happiness and appreciation from others. It's a sharing, which is based in love. When you share something that you love to do and are good at it you make the world a better place."*

HOW IT WORKS: If only everyone followed this advice money wouldn't have become the focus, the answer to everything. What happened was you got distracted at a very early age and knocked off your path before you even knew it was there. That's when the void showed up and your response was to fill it. It's all about reclaiming your life, your gifts, and talents - your destiny. It's never too late to start. Go back to your beginning and let your *spirit guides* show you the right way for you.

## *The Real Meaning of Normal*

*"You hear people say they wish their life was normal. There's even a saying for it, "Back to normal." First of all, we don't see that what they desire is normal in any way.*

*What they mean is that they want less stress in their life, they want to be loved and appreciated, they don't want to be sick or not have enough to get by. When you look at it that way, there are very few normal people. So wanting to be normal is wanting to be ordinary.*

*Ordinary people do not change the world. It's the extraordinary people – the ones who would never settle for normal that do. They follow their vision and their passion in life. What is normal is to come into this life with a purpose - a passion.*

*The passion is taken away from most people by the time they reach high school. Their dreams fade away. What they love to do and were good at gets ridiculed and the judgment makes them not pursue that vocation in life. When you look at it that way this is anything but normal."*

**HOW IT WORKS:** To be "normal" describes a safe okay life, versus a meaningful one. Your *guides* know that you came here to live out your purpose, your passions. *They* will never give up on you and that's why you will always feel a relentless yearning if you don't take action on your passions. That's *them* nudging you, reminding you.

---

# *Why You Are Here*

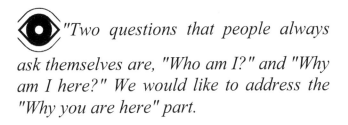*"Two questions that people always ask themselves are, "Who am I?" and "Why am I here?" We would like to address the "Why you are here" part.*

> • *You are here to observe and not judge.*
> • *You are here to listen, absorb, and process what you hear.*
> • *You are here to learn to love and be*

*loved.*

• *You are here to find and be a soul mate.*

• *You are here to help those who deserve help and learn to ask for help when you need it.*

• *You are here to realize that being grateful for what you have will prevent you from feeling envious of what you don't have.*

• *And finally, you are here to feel responsible for bringing happiness and not suffering to every living thing on the planet.*

*This is why you are here. If you follow these lessons you will never ask yourself "Why am I here?" again."*

HOW IT WORKS: Once you connect with "why you are here" the anxiety stops. That's because you stop playing the comparison game. You are paying attention and doing your part, which removes all doubt about why you are here. So if you ask yourself why you are here just realize that you got off-track somewhere along the way. Realign yourself by using your inner compass. Stop and listen to your guidance to find your way back to why you are here.

## *What Creates Your Life*

*"From our perspective, you are an awareness, a perceiver, and observer. You are an awareness that perceives. With this level of perception, you can see the influence of source in everything you observe. It's all about how you perceive what you are observing. If you have any judgment of what you observe, that is what creates your life.*

*What you observe creates feelings, emotions and beliefs, that co-create your habits. It's when people get stuck in their emotions and their feelings that the habits don't change and, therefore, your life doesn't change. It becomes a repeat day after day, week after week, and year after year. If this happens the learning stops and you spend less time in a perceptive state. Everything you perceive comes through in the moment, and once you make a*

*judgment about it the moment is gone. So what you learned or observed is now in the past.*

*The present moments tend to slip by you without you looking for the truth in them. This is how people go through decades of their life and end up wondering when they're 50, 60, 70 years old or more asking themselves, "who am I" and "why did I come here?"*

HOW IT WORKS: To be a perceiver and observer, you must live fully in the moment. The only thing that shuts it down is when the judgment starts. Do you know anyone who doesn't judge? This is why most people stay closed off to their higher potential, they are concerned about what others will think of them, as their judgment is projected back at them. Knowing that judgment is so overwhelmingly common, expect to see a lot of it. Once you detect someone judging you remove them from your circle. Free yourself to pursue your purpose in this life without interference.

# Chapter 4 - GUIDANCE REMOVES ALL STRUGGLE

## *A Worthwhile Relationship*

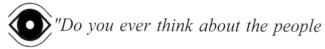*"Do you ever think about the people you hang out with? What are these people saying to you? What are they telling you to think about? Where do they take you? What do they want you to do? How do they want you to think?*

*When you look closely at your interactions with your friends and those you associate with, are these productive relationships? Shouldn't you be getting something special out of each and every relationship you have?*

*Maybe you have the same relationships you had a decade ago and you haven't learned anything new from them, or gotten beyond that circle of friends, which means you most likely haven't changed a bit. Do you view that as something positive? Probably not.*

*That empty feeling in your stomach, in your soul, is gnawing away at you, maybe for years. When you decide to have a relationship with us you will find that it is an evolving relationship that is guided by those who have your best interest in life at the forefront."*

**HOW IT WORKS:** The challenges you have been facing are now forcing you to ask these questions. This is the doorway to what really matters. If it's not authentic it doesn't matter. Everyone knows the difference now. Your *guides* are here to show you what a worthwhile relationship is. Walk with *them* as you become best friends.

## *Miracles Are Common For Us*

 *"When something unexplainable and surprisingly good happens - people call it a miracle. They refer to these occurrences as a mystery or a phenomenon. A good thing was allowed to happen.*

*Miracles are attributed to anyone other than yourself. Was it god or just a coincidence? In turn, miracles validate the existence of a higher power who grants you a miracle at his or her whim.*

*We would say that wherever love and truth reside, miracles occur naturally. We come from love and truth. We are not ever surprised by miracles, we expect them.*

*There is such an absence of love and truth in your world that you are the ones who are surprised when a miracle happens. When you live in love and truth you witness miracles every day in the most common of things."*

HOW IT WORKS: In my book, Guided, I show you how you are always being guided, even though you may not realize it. When you are guided things happen, what you may call miracles, that make your life work better than you could have done on your own. All it took was stepping into the flow at the moment you were guided to. That's how miracles really happen. They are happening all the time when you operate from an open heart of love and truth. This all becomes possible when you are more like your *guides*.

---

## *We Are Here When You Are Ready*

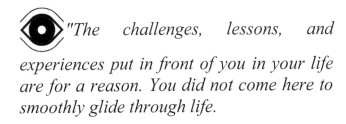*"The challenges, lessons, and experiences put in front of you in your life are for a reason. You did not come here to smoothly glide through life.*

*Your awakening is in these events, but only if you are connected. If you are not connected to the source then life happens "to" you. You learn little and you blame much in your effort to understand your suffering.*

*Walking with us as your guides brings understanding and clarity to your journey. Your life begins to happen "for" you as you stop resisting and start allowing. We are here when you are ready."*

**HOW IT WORKS:** No one is more connected to you than your *source connected guides* - no one! *They* know everything about you and why you are here. *They* are always on your side. However, *they* will never coddle you or treat you like you are helpless. *They* see doing that as stifling to the powerful being who came here to express itself in this world. This is what it's like to live a guided life with your *guides* by your side every step of the way.

---

## *You Can't Outsmart the Present Moment*

*"People spend a lot of time wishing and hoping, rather than experiencing the present moment. They look at their past and wish it would have turned out differently. They envision their future and hope that things get better for them. Doing this, they miss the most important time of their life - the present moment.*

*Your past and future are seen as being time-bound, while the present moment is not. When you are awake and alert you are in the "right now," "the right here" and paying attention to this moment is imperative.*

*If you look at the present moment under a microscope you would see infinite possibilities because that moment is a doorway to eternity. Have you ever heard of losing track of time? This happens when your total involvement is engaged in a present moment. Time disappears and you wonder where it went. You were experiencing eternity in a present moment.*

*We urge you to stop wishing and hoping, as these are failed life strategies. It's only when you immerse yourself in the present eternity that you discover yourself and your way home."*

HOW IT WORKS: The present moment is not something you control, in fact, they are the opposite of each other. You can't outsmart the present moment because the present moment is far more precise than anything you can achieve on your own. The only thing required from you is your attention, awareness, and openness to it. You have to be "on" to experience the present moment and not consumed with distractions. Your *Spirit Guide Angels* reside in the present moment and are always available to you when you ask or are open to it. Real success still awaits you. You will find it in the present moment.

## *Who Is It That's Guiding You?*

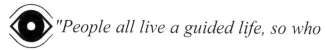 *"People all live a guided life, so who is it that's guiding you? Do you listen to the voice of conformity and social pressure, or do you listen to us?*

*We will always present you with guidance, experiences, events, and situations where you learn and grow, as well as, adapt to your current environment.*

*We never force you to do anything, nor criticize you for not doing something. Living a guided life is much more than thinking that what you have been formed and molded into doing is any way connected to who you really are and why you came here."*

**HOW IT WORKS:** Living a guided life will make you appear different to those who are disconnected from their guidance. Depending on where they are in their awareness, they may view you as either interesting or weird. Living a guided life is a co-created one. You allow your *guides* to help you so you can live a better life than you could have done on your own. It's one where anything becomes possible because you are open to it. This is what people call magic, when it's really living a guided life.

# Chapter 5 - TRUST IS NATURAL WHEN YOU KNOW YOURSELF

## *How to Look At Tragedies*

*"You should never allow your world to become so small that it is controlled by your daily rituals and activities.*

*We present you with new experiences all the time in order to expand your world and allow you to experience new things. The new things you resonate with become part of your expanding world and make your life more interesting.*

*Throughout your life, you also experience tragedy and illness. These are just parts of everyone's life. If your world is small, one of these tragedies or illnesses could break it apart into little pieces and ruin your life. That's why your world needs to be larger and not smaller.*

*Tragedies are like wildfires. They come through an area and burn everything to the ground, leaving the bare earth, a clean slate for nature to repaint. In a few years the area burned will grow back more magnificent and beautiful than ever. This is like life."*

HOW IT WORKS: The trap is that people expect things to remain the same. The moment something does change from what they were comfortable with they feel like a victim. That's misinterpreting the event or information. To prevent this - follow your guidance. Your *guides* always show you things for what they are, and you for who you are.

---

## *Everyone Big and Small Needs To "Feel Loved"*

*"All creatures have feelings no matter how big or small. Everything that feels has a sense of "I am." This sense of existence means that they naturally seek to experience happiness in their life and avoid unhappiness and suffering.*

*Lately, there's been many stories about two animals of different species who love each*

*other and get along in the wild. This is an example of that need to "feel loved," by feeling that you are needed and appreciated.*

*Man tends to have a higher intelligence level, therefore, can remember their past and think about their future. Having this higher intelligence only allows mankind to think about more "what-if's" and worry. The worrying creates fears and these fears are what keeps mankind from living a loving existence. The stress these fears cause affects man's physical and emotional well-being."*

HOW IT WORKS: The creatures in the wild are showing us how to be tolerant of the differences in each other. In fact, in spite of those differences they love and care for each other unconditionally. They don't think about the reasons why they shouldn't. They don't over-think things and freeze up. They don't procrastinate. They feel love and act on it. Could it be that they are setting an example for us? Pay attention and learn the value of reconnecting with your own primal instincts.

# *Your Awareness Is Always ON*

*"During the day your experiences come and go, but your awareness is always on.*

*A good analogy would be, when you are listening to the radio in the background as you go about your day. You have certain experiences throughout the day while the radio is playing. Occasionally you give your attention back to the radio to a song that you liked, or a news item that comes across. Your experiences and routines are interrupted by that transmission.*

*You are here to observe and learn. When messages come through from your awareness they are deliberate. Just like you could listen to a radio only in the background and not really hear it, you can miss certain guidance and transmissions from your awareness.*

*Once you realize that it's always playing then you can learn to tune out the experiences and distractions and focus on the guidance."*

HOW IT WORKS: This is a subtle shift between worlds. You are "here," but you are always receiving guidance from *them* over "there." So how do you "tune in" to your awareness, *their* guidance more often? If you are just tuning into what you want to hear, then you are not listening to your guidance. That's selective listening coming from an insecure ego. You will know it's your guidance when you get what you didn't expect, or you may not even understand it when it first comes through. Trust those transmissions coming directly from your *spirit guides*, and see how much better your life works out.

# Chapter 6 - ANXIETY - THE CONNECTION BREAKER

## *Holding Your Breath Breaks Your Connection to Us*

*"Notice when people are lost deep in thought, their breathing slows down. If they are worrying while thinking, their breathing gets even more shallow. As your mind gets more cluttered with thinking you will actually "hold your breath."*

*If you are holding your breath, one thing you will find difficult to do is to smile. Observe the people around you who rarely smile. They are shallow breathers. In the rare instance when they do smile or laugh, it's probably because they were caught "off guard" momentarily.*

*The fact that they laughed means they took a deep breath and broke the pattern. For an instant, they were brought back into the present moment where we reside. That's when they returned to their natural in-and-*

*out breathing rhythm. Their thought-worry pattern was interrupted and the mind's dominance stopped for that moment.*

*When you worry, your breath gets quiet. When you breathe your mind gets quiet."*

HOW IT WORKS: Any type of tensing up will cause you to breathe in a shallow way, and even hold your breath. Your best *advisors*, your *spirit guides*, cannot reach you when this happens because it cuts off your life-force. Think of your breath as a highway to your guidance. If you feel your breath tightening, step back, assess the situation and decide what your boundaries are. Anything that takes your breath away, breaking the connection to your *spirit guides*, needs to be eliminated from your life.

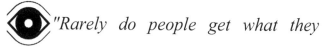

## *Staying Out of Karmic Jail*

*"Rarely do people get what they want. They may get what they need or even what they deserve at any given time, but why don't they get what they want? Do*

*they want the wrong things? People basically want the same things; a better job, more money, better friends, a better family, and all the usual stuff.*

*When they don't get what they want, they don't seem to be shaken up too much about it. Inside they may feel that it wasn't possible. This leads to not believing in themselves and having doubts. This is a symptom of low self-esteem. Next, comes not loving yourself enough.*

*Perhaps you believe in a limited universe - that there's not enough to go around for everyone, that you are competing for what it is you want? When you don't get it you may believe it's okay not to have it. What's worse is thinking it's spiritual to go without.*

*Not loving yourself enough and believing in limitations will become a karmic jail you will serve a life sentence in."*

HOW IT WORKS: What *they* are saying is that we live in an unlimited universe where everything is possible. These are not just words, it's a fact. It's also a waste of time to compete. You didn't come here to prove something to someone else. You came here to express yourself through your own creations. To do a really good job at that you need to believe in yourself. Loving yourself becomes the by-product of all that you are becoming.

## *The Source of Your Unhappiness*

*"What is the source of your unhappiness? Is it a feeling of lack or that you are not loved? We would say that your source of unhappiness is you, specifically it's your thinking. You are always thinking about yourself.*

*We are never unhappy. We do not think or worry or dwell on ourselves; we think about you. Your self-centered obsession with YOU leads to selfish beliefs and negative thoughts and emotions.*

*Self-centeredness and believing you are not connected leads to destructive thought patterns and this will damage your being. The source of happiness lies in thinking about and loving others."*

**HOW IT WORKS:** Unhappiness is centered in feeling disconnected. When you are focused on yourself you are not connected. This makes you feel like you're lacking in some way - like you're missing something, and you are! This feeling is the correct interpretation and is the notification from your inner guidance system that you need to make a course correction. That's what it feels like. It's not supposed to feel good when you are losing your way, that's how it gets your attention. Until you act on it will you actually feel connected and truly happy.

---

## Abandon Feelings of Lack

"*What are you fearful of? Are you afraid of getting old alone, or not having enough money for your retirement or even enough money right now? Are you worried about your health, your debts, paying your bills, your job, or whether or not you're good enough to have enough?*

*Of all these things, the most dangerous one is feeling that you are not enough. Your life changes when you are enough and have enough.*

*Abandoning feelings of lack brings a new perspective to your life. No longer do you see yourself as needy or as a failure. You find ways to have enough by doing things you love and with people you love to be around.*

*You will stop putting up with jobs and people you hate just to have enough money. You will begin to look at life differently. Life is not a contest of having enough to be enough."*

HOW IT WORKS: If you can't feel gratitude for who you are and what you have then you will continue to suffer from feelings of lack. It seems that the more abundance people have the more they tend to suffer from this, which makes no sense. If you feel this way you need to remove the trappings that got you off-track. Downsize, liquidate, simplify, until those feelings of lack dissipate and you reclaim yourself and your connection to everything.

# Chapter 7 - BELIEFS ARE LIKE GLASS, THEY SHATTER WHEN BROKEN

## *Why Do You Believe What You Believe?*

*"People struggle with trying to understand things. Although they may believe something, they may not understand why they believe it. This only becomes apparent to them when they try to get someone else to believe it.*

*Believing something you don't understand is something you haven't experienced yet. Once you experience it, you believe it with your heart and not your mind. On a surface level, you don't really believe or disbelieve anything.*

*When you are in the "present moment," you don't have to believe anything, it, the truth, will just reveal itself because you are fully present and listening to what we are sending you. You are listening with your heart and not your mind. This is how you discern between what you believe and what you know."*

**HOW IT WORKS:** To believe something is faith driven. To know something is experience driven. You are here, in this life, to experiment with everything. which yields experience. Only then can you really trust your decision-making. Becoming experienced can make you feel vulnerable to criticism from others. Think about how you started out in your young life to put the opinions of others into perspective. You were at the height of your life-force and nobody's opinion mattered, only the excitement of what you were experiencing. Return to that and start living again.

## *To Believe or Not to Believe*

*"When babies come into this world they have needs, but not beliefs. Needs are inherent and beliefs are something they are taught by their families, school and by the society they grow up in.*

*By the time a person reaches their 20s, they are pretty much ingrained into their beliefs. People then live the rest of their life by their beliefs. Many say they will die for their beliefs. However, the beliefs limit consciousness. Their beliefs may also keep people out of their life whom they may actually like, but can't let them into their life because of their beliefs.*

*They become someone who cannot observe anything without judgment. Their untested and unproven beliefs limit the type of experiences they have in life.*

*When you have a connection to us we present you with events that will help expand your life and provide new insight into the world without judging it first. You learn not to take things personally and see the world for what it is, maybe for the first time in your life. So release your beliefs and begin to enjoy your journey here much more."*

HOW IT WORKS: Beliefs get shattered when something else comes along that works better and makes more sense. That's why the old structures like education, the workplace, the economy, relationships and what used to be good investments are all changing or breaking. Also, that's why it's so easy to walk away from it all. This is when you begin to discover your guidance; the guidance that's always been there for you. Your *Spirit Guide Angels* are the best life coaches and advisors you could ever ask for. Having a working relationship with *them* is when you raise the bar and start living the life you intended before you got here. That's when you release the limiting beliefs and start to "live a guided life.

## *You Are Intelligent Energy Wanting to Express Itself*

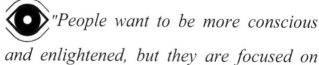 *"People want to be more conscious and enlightened, but they are focused on the wrong things. They chase something to improve themselves. The "I" as in, "I am."*

*Other things they seek outside themselves we call "this." You want "this" for the "I." We would tell you that it's much less*

*complicated than that.*

*Why do you think people greet you or say goodbye with light and love? You see, the part of you that is your essence, your consciousness, is your spirit. Your spirit doesn't need improvement and the "you" that you see in the mirror is made up of intelligent light energy. It shines brightly but is trapped inside your earth suit. So you are already enlightened. You are light and love and you are consciousness.*

*So why would you chase additional consciousness outside of who you really are, which is light energy and pure consciousness? It's not something you can get more of, but when you give it away you don't lose any of it, in fact, it multiplies! That's how it works. Light and love to you."*

HOW IT WORKS: How did people become so confused about who they are? It's because you have been conditioned to question yourself. In reality, you came here fully equipped with intelligent energy, that is until those who were already here thought they knew better and knocked you off course. To learn about your original equipment, "the intelligent energy," consult with your *spirit guides* because *they* are the experts on this.

---

## *The Yearning of Your Soul Drives the Learning*

*"The goal of receiving our guidance is self-realization. Self-realization is the urge of your non-body potential.*

*The character, the personality, your soul are who you are in the universe. To be the most effective, your learning needs to be free of pressure and coercion from outside sources like from family, friends, social and economic pressures. You must also learn to detach yourself from materialism.*

*It's the yearning of your soul that drives the learning. When you crossover your bodily senses will expire, but the real you, your soul, lives on. We're glad we could help along the way."*

HOW IT WORKS: Your *spirit guide angels* explained everything it takes to release yourself from the stuff, what anyone thinks of you, and any feelings of lack. Start small. Do something, or stop doing something, that no one but you will notice. Then pick another "need to be released item" from your list of burdens. Don't tell anyone what you are doing. Eventually, someone will take notice, but you might be surprised to see how long that actually takes while this inner shift in you is gaining strength. By the time anyone takes notice you will be way past your attachment to what they might say or do. You have earned your wings, wings that lift you up to your long-awaited potential.

## *Be Someone You Would Like To Be*

*"Why do you think people fail at what they try to accomplish? Or, if they don't fail they really didn't do it as well as they could have.*

*Did they not love themselves enough to do the job correctly? While it's easy to say you*

*should love yourself more, that's very superficial. We see it as something more elementary. We see that you don't respect yourself enough.*

*If you respected yourself you would never do just an adequate job at anything. When you don't have enough self-respect you will fall into a life of "good enough." Good enough is never good enough.*

*If you have a passion for life and everything you do, you will never settle for good enough, as it harms your self-respect. Could you love someone you didn't respect? Not likely. So what makes you think you will love yourself without the self-respect?"*

**HOW IT WORKS:** When you are fully immersed in the intensity of living your life you don't think about any of this. In fact, it's not something you think about at all. You feel the urge, step into it, and everything else takes care of itself. Everything else becomes the by-product of your actions like; respecting and loving yourself. Be someone you would like to be, someone you like and respect. Honor that above everything else no matter what the obstacles are, as this guides you to someone you really like - and that would be YOU!

# Chapter 8 - THE MEANING OF YOUR LIFE IS WHY YOU ARE HERE

## *A Meaningful Life Will Be Your Masterpiece*

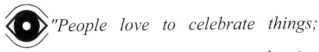 *"People love to celebrate things; birthdays, anniversaries, someone leaving their job and retiring. There are many things to celebrate.*

*What most of them have in common is cake; birthday cakes and cakes make for special occasions. It's getting together and celebrating that brings people together and helps them understand each other.*

*What do you celebrate? We would say it's your life. We didn't accompany you here to watch you earn a living. We came here with you to guide you through a meaningful life. To do this, you must look at your life like baking a cake.*

*To bake that cake, you take the best*

*ingredients and highest quality utensils and bring them together to bake your masterpiece. These ingredients are your talents, your time, your strength and effort. Each day you mix them together to create a cake, a life that's better than the day before. You do this, not for monetary gain, you do this to satisfy your soul because much of the work is lonely and hard. If you do this properly each day, abundance will be part of the reward, but that's only the icing on top of the cake."*

**HOW IT WORKS:** To create a life that's a masterpiece, you must first examine the ingredients and tools that you possess to create it. Do you have what it takes to create a masterpiece? This is where many people give up. Instead of baking a cake, start with some cupcakes. This is a metaphor to create a starting place so you don't give up before you even get started. Celebrating your life is supposed to be fun and exciting, so begin with something that's achievable. Let it be fun as you start building your masterpiece.

## *Who You Really Are You Keep Hidden*

*"A lifetime of following the rules by making yourself desirable to the marketplace and fitting into what's expected of you in society is what you have focused on perfecting. The expected reward is being liked and getting paid. Rarely does the marketplace or the society you've aligned yourself with care about who you really are.*

*The marketplace needs to fill a position that produces a profit for the company. It could even be a robot if it could fulfill the position and be a capital cost that justified itself. This is the new world you are competing in. Society wants you to follow its rules so you don't become a problem, even though it's society that goes along with the status quo that perpetuates the problems.*

*If you continue to keep yourself hidden at the expense of making yourself marketable to an entity that only cares about profits, you will become obsolete sooner than you think. These entities rely on you being a compliant citizen in society, mindlessly following the same regimen as previous generations did. That illusion has become obsolete so you no longer have to keep yourself hidden."*

**HOW IT WORKS:** Most people know what it feels like to be an employee that a company wants or expects you to be. It's called a job. It's not something you look forward to, it's something you show up for because you get paid to do it. The social norm.

Imagine getting replaced by a robot and that nightmare ending. Now, you get to come out of hiding because you no longer have any reason to be there. You did not lose a job, you were released from its bondage.

If you play your cards right you will start over before that job ends. The real motivation is not the threat of losing a j-o-b, it's getting around to living the life you intended before the nightmare began.

## *Nothing is Impossible*

*"What prevents people from accomplishing what they want in life? It's primarily having people tell them whatever they want to be or do is impossible.*

*"New people," babies, start hearing this at a very young age and it only increases as they get older. So by the time you are at your peak energy, in your late teens, you have heard it so many times that you may actually believe it.*

*You start to believe things like: "you can't do it," "it's too difficult," "it's too expensive," or "you aren't talented enough or smart enough." These kind of beliefs set the stage for the rest of your life by making you actually believe it's impossible for you to become who you came in as, who it is you really are, what you are meant to do, and why you are here.*

*We want you to look at that word you hear so many times: "Impossible," and make it into two words, "I'm Possible"...and you are!"*

**HOW IT WORKS:** Nothing is impossible if you really want it. In fact, if you REALLY want it - it's already yours. This is where employing your *guides* works like magic. *They* know how to guide you right to it, but you have to listen and take action at that moment. If you hesitate you will miss it.

---

## *The Story of Your Life*

*"The ordinary life you call boring, stressful, or lacking is the great mystery of your being here, but many try to hide from it. Why would you try to hide from your life? Ask yourself, "What am I hiding from?" Is it the commitments from my past or fears about the future?*

*You are here to live the unique life you were given and to celebrate its story. Accept gratefully what comes to you in the present moment as that is what brings real happiness. Being honest with yourself and*

*others and not taking anything that happens personally, is the way you will avoid drowning in life's daily undertow.*

*Avoid "preparing" for future outcomes. Having certain expectations about the future will limit the scope of your happiness. Like a person who wears too much cologne, there's absolutely no reason for you to cloak your life in anything "holy," "spiritual," "mysterious," "addictive," or anything else other than what it already is on its own."*

**HOW IT WORKS:** You miss the opportunities of the natural flow in the present moment when you are caught up in battling life's daily undertow. You know you're in the undertow when your life is filled with struggle. Many people are struggling because they don't know how to go about reclaiming their present moment because they are entrenched in the old ways of doing things. The consequences of stepping out of the struggle and into the flow may seem radical. However, fighting against the constant downward pull of the undertow will just beat you down. Make a radical course correction and begin living your story.

## *Live the Magic Ride of Your Life*

 *"People like to plan their life. However, most people have trouble planning their day. If you can't seem to effectively plan your day, why do you believe you can plan your life?*

*Planning is another way of hoping for a desired outcome. Looking back, how many outcomes you desired actually happened the way you planned them? So this would seem to negate the idea that planning or goal setting is effective. Plan your work and work your plan will many times run you in circles.*

*Here's what we see as more effective. Each day when you wake up you think about certain things you would like to do that day. They may be work related, or not. Instead of prioritizing lists, or labeling them as more important than another, try opening yourself up to allowing these things to happen at their own pace.*

*You may find some to be easier and almost happen by themselves. However, what you won't find is all the stress of looking at your watch and worrying about getting everything done."*

HOW IT WORKS: When I wake up in the morning I lay in the twilight between sleep and waking for about 10 to 15 minutes. This lets my *spirit guide angels* slip in *their* messages to me before I step into my day, before my feet touch the floor, grounding me back into this temporary home. Then, when I go to my office I let *them* guide me to what's really important right now. Yes, like everyone else, I have things to get done, but I also know that it will all unfold perfectly without interference from me. If you allow life to push you, you will miss the magic ride, the real fun, the pure joy of living your life, a guided one.

LINDA DEIR

# About The Author

For Linda Deir living a guided life "is" her life.

Right from the start, she met her *spirit guides*. She was just a baby when it began. Having never been separated from *them*, *they* have guided her through unimaginable circumstances, as well as her greatest successes and understandings of herself.

Throughout her life, she has followed *their* guidance and accomplished what others considered impossible. From her lifelong relationship with her *spirit guide angels*, she knows firsthand that there's nothing you can't learn, figure out, do, or have when you live a guided life.

In a world that requires people to look for answers in unconventional ways, this has never been unconventional to Linda. Her many achievements are proof that when you co-create your life with your *guides*, hence, live a guided life, you can accomplish anything. All you need to do is show up, pay attention, listen, and take action.

From the training she received from her *spirit guides* that started as a baby, she mastered living in two worlds simultaneously. What everyone in this life taught her, paled in comparison to what she learned from her *guides*.

Your *guides* don't teach you anything. *They* present you with timely events and opportunities that entice you. *They* have timing down to a science! So anything that excites you is always being sent directly from your *guides*, not just once in awhile, but all the time. This means that everything you receive has a shelf-life. *Their* timely guidance only works if you take action without hesitating. This is the most challenging part of following *their* guidance and will be critical to your success and learning. So when you feel that curiosity and wonder hit you, igniting your passions, you will know it's coming directly from your *spirit guide angels*.

The channeled insights from Linda's *spirit guide angels* presented in this book are *their* attempt to clear the path for you to make contact with your own *guides*. *They* show you how to incorporate *their* guidance into your life, creating a better life for yourself than you could have done on your own.

When *they* observe that you acted on *their* timely guidance you become a *spirit guide* magnet as *they* are attracted to the real you in action! Linda calls this the zone. You become unstoppable when you make this connection to your *source connected spirit guide angels*. Living a guided life is like stepping onto your very own yellow brick road as you connect the dots in your own life. Everything begins to make sense when you live a guided life. Let *their* messages bring you the power and clarity to make great decisions and live a fear-free guided life.

Linda and her husband and business partner, Ray Holley, channel these insights from Linda's *Spirit Guide Angels* the same way they perform all their services on their other websites: www.ChanneledReadings.com and www.LindaDeir.com

# A Note from Linda Deir

Thank you so much for reading How to Live a Guided Life, Meeting the Real YOU, Book 2, channeled from my *Spirit Guide Angels*.

Pay it forward by writing a short, helpful review of this book if it helped you or at least entertained you. Now you can help others. Do that by going to Amazon (you did not need to buy the book on Amazon to leave a review). Type "How to Live a Guided Life, Meeting the Real YOU, Book 2, channeled from my *Spirit Guide Angels* by Linda Deir" into the search field. Go down to "Write a customer review" click on it and follow the fun part of writing your review and rating it by clicking the stars.

**Linda's Weekly "Guided" Insights**: Get new insights delivered to your email box each Tuesday. Sign up at Linda's website: www.LindaDeir.com

**Coaching with Linda**: Want to talk with your *Spirit Guide Angels*? Schedule your coaching session with Linda to experience this! ~Linda Deir

# Linda's Other Books

(All of my books are available on <u>Amazon</u> in Kindle, paperback, and in audiobook format on <u>Amazon</u>, <u>Audible</u> and <u>iTunes</u>)

## GUIDED - Her Spirit Guide Angels Were Her Best Friends and Life Coaches

GUIDED is the author's true story that follows her life from survival as an abused child through her escape as a teenager and into her phenomenal success as a businesswoman in a man's world by age 19 and beyond. Using her life as a template, GUIDED is a roadmap for stepping on board at any point along your life path to join forces with your own *spirit guides* to create a better life than you could have on your own. Sprinkled throughout the book are 137 universally applicable Tips, Lessons, and Awarenesses that Linda shares directly from her life-long relationship with her *spirit guides*.

## How to Live a Guided Life, FIRST STEPS, Book 1, channeled from my Spirit Guide Angels

In this book, you will learn how to live a guided life. At any time along the way you can use this book as a reminder to keep you on your path before you stray too far off course. These reminders are your *spirit guide angels* catching you - before you slip and fall. *They* are always with you, there to catch you, and guide you...hence "Live a Guided Life."

Made in the USA
Lexington, KY
07 March 2016